AMERICAN ROOMS IN MINIATURE

by Mrs. James Ward Thorne

THE ART INSTITUTE OF CHICAGO

COVER DESIGN is from an English cotton of about
1835, printed especially for the American trade

Eighth Edition

Reprinted 1980

Printed by Hillison & Etten Co., a division of John Blair & Company

Designed by Everett McNear

ISBN 0-86559-001-X

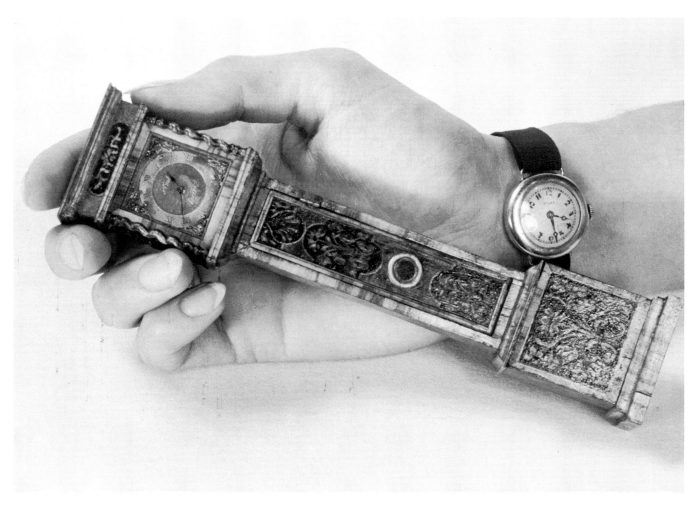

*The Miniature Rooms are built to a uniform scale
of one inch to the foot, making them
one-twelfth actual size. The illustration shows
the comparative size of one of the pieces.*

FOREWORD

THIS GROUP OF MINIATURE ROOMS, generously presented to The Art Institute of Chicago in 1942 by its inspired author, consists entirely of American interiors and gives an unusually complete survey of the development of domestic interior design in this country from the seventeenth century to the present. It is indeed a fully developed American Wing in miniature which in its full scale equivalent would require a larger area for its display than is at present given for this purpose in any museum in the country not devoted entirely to Americana.

In many instances the rooms are reproductions or reconstructions of famous examples, some intimately connected with the lives of famous Americans—Washington, George Mason, Andrew Jackson, etc., which no one institution could ever hope to assemble under its roof in the original. Even though the exigencies of a "three wall" representation have in general forced certain departures from literal correctness, every effort has been made to preserve and emphasize the spirit of the room and to render it in accurate scale.

Few if any such rooms as they now exist contain any of their original furnishings. Whenever happy circumstances have preserved some of them, reproductions of these pieces have been used in the model and in every case the interiors have been completed with furnishings of the type which in all probability adorned them during the days of their greatest glory. In several instances the furniture used in the model is not contemporary with that in fashion when the original room was built. In these cases it is generally later, sometimes by as much as a generation. In one or two models representing originals of a delayed type the furnishings follow this conservative lead. By no means all of the furniture originally used in such rooms was of American origin for it must be remembered, as proved by historical record, that particularly during the eighteenth century along the Atlantic coast the wealthy planter and his merchant contemporary were in close contact with England whence came luxuries in exchange for raw materials. It is probable that even in the simpler houses pieces of English origin found their place with the products of the local craftsmen. American furniture came to differ as it did from its English sources in the same measure as the manners and accent of the colonists themselves.

Some of these miniature interiors are not copies of single originals but have been assembled according to data provided by several extant or recorded examples. This has been done in cases where no single surviving example was sufficiently representative of the type as a whole and where the importance of the type was not sufficient to warrant several examples.

Models such as these, in spite of their necessary limitations, some of which are by no means obvious, are in many ways superior to the so-called "period room" for presenting a complete picture of a type or style in its entirety. They offer a flexibility of lighting, setting and furnishing which the actual period room with its demands of piece by piece authenticity, its spatial requirements and the exigencies of lighting and accessibility, can never approach. Supplemented by displays of original objects and furniture, they would seem to offer an ideal solution of the hitherto unsolved problem of an adequate three-dimensional demonstration of the arts of decoration in the public museum.

Mrs. Thorne's solution of the problem of scale in these rooms is almost magical. While recognizing that an absolute solution is practically beyond human capacity, she has succeeded to an unprecedented degree in relating each part so that a feeling of complete consistency has been attained. While in earlier series the majority of the tiny objects used were the result of years of collecting, in these rooms most of them were actually made to scale for their particular places. Special processes were developed for obtaining a hair-line fineness in moldings and ornament and even the textiles were specially prepared in many instances to give the faery delicacy demanded.

The present series consists of thirty-seven units. These can be roughly divided into three groups. The first illustrates the developments which took place in the North Atlantic region from the settlements on Massachusetts Bay to the days of the "brownstone front." The second shows the more spacious if less precise attainments of the Old Dominion and her neighbors to the south. The third takes up the nineteenth century types of the Middle West, the antebellum Deep South, the Southwest, and California with her Spanish traditions and latest cosmopolitanism.

The models are all built to a scale of one inch to one foot, making them one-twelfth of the size of the original. They exhibit the combined skill and experience of a corps of expert craftsmen who developed their unique abilities under Mrs. Thorne's direction over a period of more than a decade.

The date given in the title of each unit is in general that of the construction of the original as nearly as can be ascertained. When the room is not a reproduction but a construction of typical elements this date covers the period so represented. This is indicated by the letter (T).

This handbook was prepared by Meyric B. Rogers; the text is based on material furnished by Mrs. Thorne.

1. LIVING ROOM AND KITCHEN
EARLY MASSACHUSETTS HOUSE (T)
1675-1700

When the Pilgrim fathers landed in Plymouth in 1620 they contrived only the crudest shelters for their families but in the course of a few decades they were able to build simple yet comfortable homes recalling in form and structure those they had left behind in England. The kitchen was the common living room which sometimes served every purpose, the daily life of the family centering around its great open fireplace. After dark the room was dimly lighted by home-made candles, reeds soaked in grease, or small iron "Betty" lamps in which a wick floated in oil.

Kitchen utensils were of the simplest order. Glass and pottery in general use in Europe were largely replaced in these infant settlements by sturdier pewter plates and mugs, and wooden bowls and trenchers.

In spite of many unreliable though proud traditions regarding early importations, the furniture was at first probably only of the simplest necessities. A little later pieces corresponding to those in use in comfortable English homes began to appear. Among these were the chest and its variations and the settle, a bench with a high back extending to the floor to keep drafts from the neck and feet. Chairs were a rarity, stools and benches being the usual seat. The armchair was a seat of honor. Here two examples are shown, both of historic interest. The first, of many turned spindles, follows an example traditionally belonging to Elder Brewster, one of the leaders of the Mayflower settlement. The second is named after Governor Carver, also of the Plymouth Colony.

The bedrooms which also served as withdrawing rooms or parlors usually contained little more than a large bed, a cradle and a trundle-bed for older children. The latter was built low on small wooden wheels permitting it to be pushed under the parents' bed during the day. A chest or two, some stools and small tables were probably all that even the most elaborate bedrooms of the time contained in addition.

Floor coverings of which the braided mat is the earliest recorded were probably of great rarity. The floors of the kitchen were usually sanded in accord with the custom of the day which enabled easy disposal of refuse.

The exterior of these early houses was marked by an interesting overhang of the second story. This structural feature was emphasized decoratively by drops or pendants such as may be seen here through one of the windows.

This model was developed by combining interesting features of the Parson Capen house in Topsfield, Massachusetts, and an early room now in the Concord Antiquarian Society. The Capen house, built in 1683, is one of the finest surviving examples of American seventeenth century architecture.

2. PARLOR

THIS INTERESTING New England room is installed in the American Wing of the Metropolitan Museum. The house was built in 1671 and altered in 1710 when the paneled wall and "double hung" windows were added.

This sturdy low-ceiled type of construction was well planned for the northern shores where winters were long and intensely cold. The warm glow of the Indian red paint, the low-beamed ceiling and the big open fireplace must have offered a cheery welcome to a frost-nipped wayfarer. Incidentally the house served for many years as an inn or tavern.

The paneling is English in feeling which makes one realize that the housewrights who built in this new America worked with a memory of houses they knew in the home country. Their ideal was to reproduce these Old World houses as accurately as possible. This holds true also of the furniture. Many of America's first settlers had been familiar in England with furniture of comfort and beauty. With the nostalgia natural to the emigrant they tried to copy these things in their new homes. Today this is spoken of as "memory furniture" and although the workmanship is sometimes faulty and more crude than the Old World pieces, it has a definite native flavor.

At the left of this model room is a paneled New England court cupboard, Jacobean in character, yet it has a distinct American quality. The stiles of the "cup-borde" have split spindle decoration, a substitute for the massive carving which was used so extensively on Renaissance furniture in Europe.

The "wainscot" chair near the fireplace is an American version of an English model. This seat of honor gave the craftsman an opportunity to show his skill in woodcarving, but it was too costly and elaborate to be popular. The stool, side chair and day bed of a later type are richly carved and have caned seats and backs. These are typical of the Restoration period in England after 1660.

Bright India prints were popular during Colonial days. They were used as table covers, bedspreads and curtains. The small chair beside the center table is covered with "Turkey work" embroidery so popular in seventeenth century England. The knitting on the table is actually worked on celluloid needles made the size of a pin.

3. DINING ROOM
SALEM, MASSACHUSETTS (T)
EARLY 18TH CENTURY

DURING THE EARLY YEARS of the Colonies, fishing was the great industry of New England. This developed ship-building, especially of small fishing vessels. Salem became the center of this activity and here were built the great whaling fleets which brought fortunes to their Yankee owners from the Newfoundland Banks. Later the ships of Salem sailed around the Horn, returning with cargoes of spices and chests of rich silks, rare porcelains and fine old Chinese rugs to adorn the homes of Salem's affluent merchant captains.

The houses of these prosperous Salem citizens were built by local workmen trained to the exacting standards of the shipwrights. As architectural aids these builders had English books such as the "Builder's Companion" and "The Young Carpenter's Assistant," but they had to depend largely upon native ingenuity in adapting these designs to native materials and practices.

This model of a dining room was inspired by the design of a paneled room in the venerable and historic Turner-Ingersoll house. Built in 1668, this house is externally of an earlier type, but inside it bears the stamp of several later alterations.

The type of paneling shown here was very popular in the New England Colonies during the first years of the eighteenth century. Such woodwork with cupboards and decorative pilasters was built into the more primitive rooms of many of the early dwellings to adjust them to the demands of later standards.

Nathaniel Hawthorne used the Ingersoll house as the scene of his famous romance, "The House of Seven Gables." It contains a secret staircase which adds to its quaint charm.

The tiny blue and white porcelains which decorate this small model were made in China and the various types of chairs give interesting examples of American designs in the William and Mary style. The inlaid walnut side table, highboy and clock are copied from American-made pieces, though also following closely the English styles of the previous quarter century.

The floor is covered with a remarkable reproduction of an old Chinese rug such as might have been brought to Salem in the East Indian trade.

4. PARLOR
CONNECTICUT VALLEY TAVERN (T)
ABOUT 1750

THE ARCHITECTURE that developed along the Connecticut River followed in general the New England type but in certain details, particularly in the treatment of the main entrances and the fireplace paneling, a very distinctive regional type was evolved. The reasons for this are not altogether clear but in the latter case it may have come from the endeavor of eighteenth century owners of older houses with low ceilings to "modernize" the appearance of these rooms with an adaptation of the more monumental features which were then in vogue and avoid the expense of rebuilding. The free and playful designs that resulted are particularly charming, offering an intimacy which is unique for the period and consequently much imitated in modern revivals.

In order to give the full flavor of this work, the model has been assembled from two actual examples. The corner cupboards follow those from the Harrison-Linsley house in Branford and the fireplace paneling is taken from the Mather house in Lyme, now demolished. This is the reason for the two kinds of pilasters, both typical with the characteristic rosettes below the capitals, and hardly more than ornamental reflections of their classic models. Another feature most distinctive of the Connecticut Valley is the curvilinear headings of the panels which seem to have been copied from the furniture designs of the late seventeenth century. The mantel with its frieze and shelf is unusual and may have been a later alteration since usually the fire opening was framed with a single bold molding with no shelf.

The furniture is very simple as befitting the parlor of a tavern, the taproom of which may be seen through the side door. The Windsor chairs show both English and American types, the settee and desk chair being definitely Colonial. The ornaments in the cupboards are painstaking copies of Staffordshire and Rockingham of the "cottage" type after examples in American collections. A certain license has been taken here since many of these like the steamer print on the wall are of nineteenth century origin.

It should be noted that in existing examples the arrangement of the paneling is hardly ever as symmetrical as it is shown here.

5. DRAWING-ROOM
JEREMIAH LEE MANSION, MARBLEHEAD, MASSACHUSETTS
1768

FISHER FOLK of the English Channel Islands, appreciating the unusual advantages of Marblehead Harbor, settled there and built comfortable dwellings in this windswept New England town perched high upon a rocky headland. The fishing industry developed rapidly and Marblehead entered upon a period of great prosperity. Commodious and imposing homes were built by wealthy ship owners and merchants. Outstanding among these was the Lee Mansion erected in 1768 by Colonel Jeremiah Lee at what was then the enormous cost of ten thousand English pounds. In the following period the Lee home was the center of Marblehead social activity for the Colonel and his wife were hospitable and noted for their generosity and public spirit. Often the great rooms echoed with music and laughter as the flickering candles shone upon men and women in powdered wigs and colorful brocades. In the Boston Museum of Fine Arts can be seen today portraits of Colonel Lee and his wife in just such distinguished attire.

The richly paneled drawing-room of the Lee Mansion reflects the continued influence of the noted English architect, Sir Christopher Wren. It is said that the wallpaper and interior woodwork of the house were executed in England and shipped to Marblehead in the Colonel's own vessels. However this may be, the elaborate carving of the mantel and overmantel in this room shows the direct inspiration of Abraham Swan's "British Builder" with its later modifications of the Wren tradition. The hallway with its imposing staircase and walls decorated with beautiful scenic paper is a distinguished example of the classical fashion of that time.

This eighteenth century house, considered one of the fine examples of Colonial architecture, is now a museum. It is not adequately furnished at present and therefore this miniature model does not contain reproductions of the pieces one sees scattered about the fine old rooms today. The mansion was built when Queen Anne furniture was still disputing Chippendale innovations in the Colonies. Since the room itself shows a predilection for an early eighteenth century style it is not unsuitable for the furniture, even the importations, to show a like feeling. The secretary and clock are rare pieces of small-scale furniture made of old burl walnut, exact replicas of old English pieces. The clock opens and winds. Every drawer of the secretary opens and even the secret drawers are reproduced.

The needlepoint rug is copied from an old English design. The brass side brackets and chandelier are copies of contemporary pieces and polished to a mirror-like brilliance in the eighteenth century fashion.

6. DINING ROOM
WENTWORTH GARDNER HOUSE, PORTSMOUTH, NEW HAMPSHIRE
1760

THE EXTERIOR of this house is considered to represent the best of the mid-eighteenth century Georgian of the northern Colonies; the interior reflects the dignity and charm of the eighteenth century homes of Portsmouth.

The entrance hall is the glory of the house. The delicate spindles of the stairway and other intricate ornament were worked by some of the remarkable carvers who were employed in the local shipyards.

The dining room is simpler in architectural detail but it has an unusual corner cupboard, a fine cornice and well designed paneling. The scenic wallpaper, after a series printed in Paris by Dufour and Leroy in 1824, represents a period later than the building of the room itself, though its fine greys add much to its beauty. Wallpaper came early to the Colonies from France and England. There are records of its sale from 1712 on. The popularity of this mural decoration and the high cost of its importation encouraged American reproduction and in 1739 Plunket Fleeson of Philadelphia manufactured the first wallpapers made in this country.

The furniture, Chippendale in character, consists of reproductions of fine American examples. The Lowestoft and blue and white china in the cupboard are copied in miniature from objects in a famous American collection. The rug is a needlepoint copy of Oriental design.

Above the fireplace hangs a hatchment, a large framed painting of the family coat of arms, which was hung outside on the front door when death occurred in a household. Many Colonial families held to this English custom.

The small pieces of silver plate on the sideboard are particularly fine in quality and execution though somewhat later in style than the other furniture.

The Wentworth Gardner house is the property of The Society for the Preservation of New England Antiquities, and is open to the public during the summer months.

7. ENTRANCE HALL

PEIRCE MANSION, PORTSMOUTH, NEW HAMPSHIRE

1799

WHEN JOHN PEIRCE built his home in Portsmouth, its stateliness and beauty earned for it the term mansion; and down through many generations that name has held.

Although there are no documents to prove it, this house is believed to be the work of Charles Bulfinch, the Boston architect, who is credited with designing a number of buildings in this maritime city.

There is great delicacy in the carving of the interior woodwork of the mansion. The cornice of the hall, the fluted pilasters, and the extreme simplicity of line and form are almost modern in feeling though the house was built one hundred and forty years ago.

The formal design of the entrance to a room under the soffit of the stairs is a clever and unique contrivance.

The mahogany settee of Hepplewhite lines, made to fit in the curve of the stairway, is copied from the original piece used in the hall today. This settee was undoubtedly designed for the place, possibly by the architect of the house, for it seems to be an integral part of the hallway.

As a rule the floors of the finer houses of the late Colonial period were covered with Oriental rugs. These were brought to England as early as the sixteenth century and were later sent to America. During the last half of the eighteenth century needlework rugs reached their zenith of popularity in England, so it is natural to suppose that they, too, were much in demand in the Colonies and were ordered from the mother country with furniture, silver, rich damasks and other luxuries. The texture of these needlework rugs was so delicate that they did not survive the hard usage of several generations and so today old examples are very rare.

Portsmouth boasts of many fine homes of citizens who have been the backbone of American industry and it is justly proud of this record.

8. BEDROOM
OAK HILL, PEABODY, MASSACHUSETTS
ABOUT 1800

AT THE BEGINNING of the nineteenth century when Samuel McIntire reached the zenith of his career, Salem was also at the height of its prosperity. There was much activity in residential construction and in consequence many fine examples of McIntire's work exist in and around the city.

McIntire's style in conformity with the fashion of the times was strongly classic. Like his younger contemporary, Charles Bulfinch of Boston, he studied Palladio whose book was in his library, and was greatly influenced by the English classicists, especially Robert Adam who advocated austerity of form with great delicacy of detail. Both as a designer and carver of ornament and furniture, for he was both architect and craftsman, he was well able to live up to these requirements as he had a fine training from his father who was also a wood carver and cabinetmaker.

In spite of these influences his style is distinctive and it is not difficult to recognize it in the garlands, sheaves of wheat and baskets of flowers with which he decorated his furniture and his mantels, doorheads and cornices. These were either carved or cast in a special composition.

The original of this model was formerly in Oak Hill, designed by McIntire for Captain Nathaniel West and particularly for his wife, Elizabeth Derby West, the daughter of Elias Hasket Derby, McIntire's chief client. Mrs. West was a lady of taste and closely supervised the designing of most of the furniture for her home.

The furniture now used in the room and reproduced in part in this model came mostly from the Derby and West families and was therefore actually part of the original scheme. The bed, the painted side chairs and many other pieces including the superb bowfront commode and mirror by the Boston cabinetmaker, John Seymour, are masterpieces of their kind.

The original of this room and two others from Oak Hill are now preserved in the Boston Museum of Fine Arts.

Through the window of the model may be seen the reproduction of an exterior designed by McIntire.

9. PARLOR
EAGLE HOUSE, HAVERHILL, MASSACHUSETTS
1818

IN THE EIGHTEENTH and early nineteenth centuries most of the New England merchants acquired their wealth through shipping. They sent their vessels to the West Indies and Europe and as far as India and China. Many an enterprising lad shipped in his early 'teens and by his thirties was not only a captain but an owner, able to build himself a fine house for which his own ships brought at his order the porcelains of Canton, wallpaper and damask from France and fine furniture from England. The parlor from Eagle House is a beautiful example of an interior from such a merchant's home of the Federal period.

The woodwork shows the fine scale detail characteristic of the time, the ornament carried out either in composition or cut with a gouge and drill. Designs of this type are generally inspired by carpenters' and builders' handbooks such as that of Asher Benjamin and charmingly emphasize the quality of the materials used. Very slender engaged or free-standing colonnettes are almost distinctive of the style.

The furniture reflects the relative elegance and luxury with which the prosperous New England merchant was able to surround his life; but a certain austerity is also evident in the clean slenderness of the lines of these American adaptations of the fashionable designs of Hepplewhite and Sheraton. The direct influence of the former is shown in the shield back chair, and Sheraton designs are the source of the high-backed armchair and sofa. On each side of the tambour desk is a delicate candle stand holding a silver stick which in those days took the place of our modern floor lamp. On the wall beside the bookcase are two rarely beautiful gilded girandoles or candle sconces with inset convex mirrors. The originals in full scale are in the Metropolitan Museum of New York. The remaining pieces, the fire screen and tables, are all replicas of period examples.

Through the windows may be seen an eighteenth century New England Town Common in winter time.

The original room is now to be seen in the American Wing of the Metropolitan Museum of Art in New York City, though in this model another old scenic wallpaper design has been used and other changes made in the furnishings.

10. DINING ROOM
HARRISON GRAY OTIS HOUSE, BOSTON, MASSACHUSETTS
1795

Harrison gray otis owned three handsome residences in Boston during his lifetime. All were distinguished designs in the late Georgian style built for him by Charles Bulfinch, Boston's outstanding architect of the early Federal period between 1795 and 1807.

Bulfinch was born in America in 1763. His parents were wealthy and he was given unusual opportunities during his youth. After studying at Harvard he traveled extensively in France and Italy where he cultivated a taste for architecture. Upon his return to Boston he studied classical design and his work is known today for its fine proportions and the refinement of its detail.

The house of which the dining room is here reproduced was the first residence built by Bulfinch* for Mr. Otis. It is now the headquarters of the Society for the Preservation of New England Antiquities, an organization to which New Englanders and Americans in general owe a great debt of gratitude for its painstaking care of treasures of the past which would otherwise have been destroyed.

In planning the interior of the Otis house Bulfinch followed the trend set by the English architect, Robert Adam, some decades earlier. The mantel and doorheads of the dining room are classical in type and are treated with the utmost delicacy and restraint. The woodwork and walls are painted in three tones of Wedgwood green, giving a cameo quality to the carving.

It is said that Mr. Otis had fine taste and bought for his homes the best that England and America could offer. The pieces of furniture made in miniature to furnish this model are of a type which was most popular in England when Robert Adam was at the height of his influence. This furniture is Hepplewhite in style and executed in pear wood inlaid in darker woods.

The needlework rug is Georgian in character, copied from a fine example in The Art Institute of Chicago. The silver was made by London silversmiths. The candle sconces and mirror over the mantel are reproduced from a very fine set owned by the Philadelphia Museum of Art.

It should be noted that the model does not follow the actual room in its arrangement, some features having been transposed in order to give a clearer idea of the spirit of the room in the three walls available. The windows in the original are closer spaced and have twelve instead of fifteen lights or panes.

*The attribution to Bulfinch is now questioned.

11. PARLOR
WATERMAN HOUSE, WARREN, RHODE ISLAND
ABOUT 1820

DURING THE EARLY nineteenth century, a period of great prosperity for this region, the Rhode Island towns of Warren and Bristol evolved a distinctively local architecture. The Waterman House in Warren is a characteristic example of the type which combines earlier features such as the broken reverse curve pediment with detail derived from the Adam style. The architect, Russell Warren of Bristol, was the leader in this development and, like John Holden Greene of Providence, was responsible for many of the finest houses and public buildings of Rhode Island between 1800 and 1830.

The delicate yet bold detail of the mantel and doorheads is here particularly noteworthy. The treatment of the dado is also unusually elaborate and varied. The ornament is based principally on Adam motifs of garlands, bowknots and floral swags but combined in a way that is definitely American and individual.

Due to the need for condensation but in violation of actualities, the door at the rear of the model opens into a hallway showing a classical entrance door with delicate fanlight and side lights, a scheme so popular in the New England states. In conformity with the times both Warren and Greene frequently used plastered walls unbroken from baseboard to cornice, and as a result paper and stenciled designs became the usual means of decorating wall surfaces. The walls of this hallway are stenciled in a most interesting design of the period.

About fifty years previously in Newport, Rhode Island, John Goddard had developed a style of furniture which raised him to the top rank of American cabinetmakers. He produced handsome block front desks, secretaries, chests and bonnet-topped highboys with bracket feet and bold shell carving. Two very fine examples of his work have been copied for this room. The chairs are distinguished types of American Chippendale as is the mirror between the windows. The rug is a needlepoint copy of an Oriental design.

12. LIVING ROOM
CAPE COD COTTAGE (T)
1750-1850

Cape cod proper and the adjacent islands of Martha's Vineyard and Nantucket, while part of New England, have an individuality both geographical and cultural which sets them apart. Though the Pilgrims touched at Provincetown, they settled on the mainland. The "Cape" was relatively poor land and unattractive to the farmer. It was settled slowly and mainly by people who turned naturally to the sea, as fishermen and sailors. Even when whaling and overseas commerce brought wealth to the great mainland ports, the prosperity of the Cape was only moderate.

These conditions are expressed in its buildings and houses. The typical example is the one-story cottage, small and compactly planned as the boats built by the same craftsmen. All attempt at display is lacking and even the paneled partitions around the "companionway" stairway and central chimney are reduced to the simplest necessities. Their charm lies wholly in an instinctively good proportion and a fitness to the place and purpose.

Without following any particular example or even the typical arrangement of windows and doors, this model gives the flavor of these homes of the Cape fisher folk as they appeared during the first half of the last century and in many instances, practically to the present.

The furniture is extremely simple, a mixture of eighteenth and nineteenth century pieces. Nothing is of outstanding merit but the effect is of a restful and intimate comfort not unlike that of a snug boat. The "butterfly" table beneath the window, the Windsor chair and the modified "Sheraton" desk are all representative items that might well have been in such a room during the first half of the nineteenth century and still make perfect equipment for a summer home. Much pains have been taken to obtain typical ornaments and prints sufficiently accurate and minute for this model, even to a miniature bottle and a still more miniature ship within.

Through the door are hollyhocks and a glimpse of the neighboring house. Through the window is the distant Atlantic, the eternal background of the Cape.

The necessity for showing several features typical of these cottages has brought about an arrangement which would hardly be found in any one room. A certain liberty has been taken by the introduction of a bayed window instead of the practically universal double-hung sash.

13. BEDROOM
NEW ENGLAND (T)
1750-1850

THIS MODEL has no definite ancestry and its arrangement follows no architectural limitations, being a construction of features common to all of the New England states assembled to give best the atmosphere of what may be called the traditional bedroom.

It does, however, answer one question. In the absence of paneling and the scarcity of wallpaper before the middle of the nineteenth century, how did the housewife relieve the bareness of plaster walls? Careful investigation of old houses has provided the solution—the stencil. With some ingenuity and patience the simple units of a stencil cut-out could be and were constructed to give such charming effects as shown here. This pattern was found in the Abner Goodall home in Marlborough, Massachusetts, on a wall surface back of an old cupboard where it had been hidden for years and preserved intact. It dates probably from the first quarter of the nineteenth century, possibly earlier, though the fact that these patterns were traditional and the work of itinerant journeymen makes a precise date impossible.

The simple partition paneling and broad floor boards suggest the second half of the eighteenth century. The furniture of maple and painted beech ranges from types of the early eighteenth century to about 1840 when the "Boston" rocker and sewing table appeared.

The corner washstand with its bowl and pitcher suggests life when the modern bathroom was unknown.

14. DRAWING-ROOM
ANDALUSIA, BENSALEM TOWNSHIP, PENNSYLVANIA
REMODELLED 1834-1836

U P TO THE EARLY eighteenth century "classic" architecture had followed more or less closely the ideas of Andrea Palladio, an Italian scholar and architect of the sixteenth century. The publication of the first volume of a work on Greek architecture by Stuart and Revett in 1762 began a new phase, the "Greek Revival," which in America, under the added impetus of the drive for a truly "republican" architecture fostered by Thomas Jefferson and the work of Benjamin Latrobe and William Thornton, was developed into almost a national style. The Greek Revival was not only the reason for the columned portico and the temple facade, but also for city names such as Athens, Sparta and Syracuse which appeared with the first stages of the westward expansion of the new nation.

In its more developed phases this style in England was largely governed by the work of Sir John Soane, the architect of the famous Bank of England, who adapted the Adam and French "Empire" styles to this new interest, which in furniture was also reflected in the later designs of Thomas Sheraton.

The room was probably part of the remodelling of an older house undertaken by Nicholas Biddle at the height of the movement. Architecturally it shows the influence of the Soane manner and the taste for stronger color contrasts which came with the Empire style.

The furnishings are of the late Sheraton-Empire type also known as the Regency style in England. This was given a distinctive interpretation in this country particularly in the work of Duncan Phyfe, a New York cabinetmaker of Scotch birth and training whose models are largely followed in these miniature reproductions. Phyfe's furniture is notable for the quality of its workmanship and its excellent use of the mahogany of which it is made as well as the marked individuality of its design.

The settee is after a design by Samuel McIntire of Salem, Phyfe's contemporary, who worked in a similar manner.

The "bull's-eye" sconces or mirrored wall brackets are copies of examples in the Metropolitan Museum, New York City.

15. PARLOR
28 EAST 20th STREET, NEW YORK CITY
1850-1875

DURING THE THIRD QUARTER of the nineteenth century fashionable life in New York City centered on Madison Square. Fifth Avenue from Washington Square to the early thirties was lined with the newer mansions of the wealthy. On the side streets to the east and west were rows of so-called "brownstone fronts" where lived the main body of what then constituted New York society. These blocks of houses were nearly all alike, three or four stories in height with English basements and stone steps mounting from the sidewalk to a heavy paneled front door on the first floor. In the days of their glory, a pull at the bell of almost any of these houses would have brought a tinkle in the basement kitchen below and soon the door would have been opened by a maid in long sweeping skirts and a stiffly starched, beruffled apron and cap.

It was in such a Victorian house at 28 East 20th Street that President Theodore Roosevelt spent his childhood. Anyone who has visited this shrine will recognize in this model the blue curtains, grey wallpaper and the mantel with its imposing gilt mirror.

Tradition assures us that a rubber plant was in every front window. Here as in parlors of the affluent were the fashionable sets of chairs, sofas and tables from the shop of Mr. John Henry Belter. Belter's elaborately carved rosewood furniture, pierced and high-crested like a Spanish comb, was the fashionable successor to the more classic designs of Duncan Phyfe.

Although for many years this period of decoration has been stamped with disapproval, here and there we see fine examples of this nineteenth century rococo furniture used in interesting new settings. The heavy, ornate quality of Victorian design makes it at times an interesting contrast to the stark simplicity of modern decoration or lack of it.

16. DRAWING-ROOM
MOUNT PLEASANT, PHILADELPHIA, PENNSYLVANIA
1761

OF ALL THE CITIES of the Atlantic Colonies, Philadelphia has bequeathed to us the most ornamentally developed architecture and the richest furniture. Among the eighteenth century houses still standing, none has greater beauty of design or more historic interest than Mount Pleasant built for John Macpherson and later owned by Benedict Arnold and his gay and beautiful wife. This distinguished house reflects the luxury and elegance of the English Georgian period for, during the middle of the eighteenth century, many English carvers and craftsmen migrated to America and settled in Philadelphia where they set a very high standard of skilled workmanship and were extensively patronized by the wealthy fashionables called "the worldly folk" by the plain-living Quakers.

The room here reproduced is really a composite of several rooms in Mount Pleasant. The design of the mantel and its flanking cupboards is typically Philadelphian in its elegance and exquisite detail. The pale raspberry tone on walls and woodwork follows one of the original colors used in 1761.

Mount Pleasant has plain ceilings, but in order to show an example of rococo plasterwork so characteristic of Philadelphia houses, the ornate rocaille design on the drawing room ceiling of the famous Powel House now in the Philadelphia Museum was selected for reproduction.

In Philadelphia after 1750 the finest walnut and mahogany furniture was built and richly carved by such cabinetmakers as Benjamin Randolph, William Savery, and Jonathan Gostelowe. They developed a style and character of work which has been given the name "Philadelphia Chippendale" because its design was derived in part from the engravings published by Thomas Chippendale in "The Gentleman and Cabinetmaker's Director." These American artisans introduced a monumentality and elegance into their furniture which lifts it to the top rank of pre-Revolutionary craftsmanship in this country. The pieces of furniture used in this room are reproductions in miniature of the finest examples of this type.

Mount Pleasant is now administered by the Philadelphia Museum of Art and is open to the public.

17. GREAT HALL
THE MILLER'S HOUSE, MILLBACH, PENNSYLVANIA
1752

"PENNSYLVANIA DUTCH" is a term used to designate those colonists from the Rhineland, mostly German, and members of the Mennonite, Amish, Moravian, and Dunker sects who settled near Philadelphia and along the Delaware and Susquehanna Rivers during the early eighteenth century. In traveling through that part of the state today one sees their rough stone houses and great red barns, the latter often elaborately decorated with "hexenfoos" devices. It is their belief that these circular discs and stars painted in gay colors protect stock and grain from the machinations of evil spirits. The same "hexes" form the designs painted on the furniture inside their homes.

This model of a kitchen or great hall is copied with certain rearrangements from the house of Jerg Muler of Millbach built in Lebanon County in 1752. Two rooms from this house are now in the Philadelphia Museum.

There are several interesting features to this room. The mantel beam, nearly ten feet long, is hewn from one piece of oak. The corner staircase and the raised and carved panels of the door are unusually handsome. The double-cock wrought-iron hinges of the latter are peculiar to the region.

For their furniture the German settlers used pine and oak. Elaborately decorated open dressers were crowded with pewter, brass and pottery. This brilliant, highly glazed pottery was manufactured in Pennsylvania. Its rich green and red clay tones add their color to that of the chests, dressers and cupboards generally painted with gay and interesting designs, many of these being developments of the "hex" symbols. Almost without exception the furniture shows how closely these settlers kept to the folkways they brought with them from the Old World. These German and Swiss designs are unmistakable. Before the open fire are many household objects made at the village forge.

On the large center table is a decorated glass copied from an example of Stiegel glass owned by the Metropolitan Museum of New York. About 1765 Heinrich Stiegel, a German by birth, settled in Lancaster County, Pennsylvania, and began the manufacture of this distinctive type of glassware which he painted with flowers and birds or engraved delicately after the German fashion.

On the small candle stand is a pewter "Betty" lamp of Pennsylvania German design.

The "Dutch" housewife wished no rugs cluttering her immaculate sandstoned floors. She loved her garden which most naturally abounded in Old World flowers of all varieties.

18. LIVING ROOM
SHAKER COMMUNITY HOUSE (T)
ABOUT 1800

THE UNITED SOCIETY of Believers in Christ's Second Appearing, commonly known as the "Shakers," were an offshoot of the English Quakers. Under the leadership of Ann Lee, a branch of the Society was established in this country in 1774 with headquarters at New Lebanon, New York. The name came from the spasmodic movements with which the members of the sect expressed their religious fervor.

During the early nineteenth century the sect spread into Pennsylvania, Ohio, Kentucky, and Indiana, each community establishing its own code of regulations, but the basis of celibacy and close communal living which were fundamental tenets made its ultimate disappearance inevitable without the backing of a larger universal organization such as aided other monastic communities.

Their devoted adherence to their principle of life, "Hands to work and hearts to God," did, however, create a highly individualized culture which emphasized an economy, directness and honesty of craftsmanship which was not without effect upon surrounding communities.

The "Believers" lived a communal life in huge barn-like buildings, avoiding all display and working like the best medieval craftsmen chiefly for the glory of God. The women attended to household duties while the men cultivated the land and worked in the shops; for the ideal of each community was to be absolutely self-supporting.

Deprived of any ornamental outlet, the craft spirit of the Shakers expressed itself in attention to proportion and fitness to purpose. The later communities in Kentucky and Ohio relaxed sufficiently to permit the use of color, using blue woodwork and painting the furniture in dull red, mustard yellow and green.

In order to show the essential characteristics of Shaker production in a condensed form, the model follows an interior constructed after the Shaker plan by an eminent authority on the cult to provide a setting for a unique collection of its furniture and crafts.

On one side of the dining room table are the seats of the brothers, on the other, those of the sisters. At the double desk are two identical chairs presumably for the business affairs of the two component parts of the community. The broad brimmed hats on the rack indicate part of the uniform of the men and the bonnet in course of construction, that of the women. The vases of flowers are a concession to "vanity" which Ann Lee would probably have found displeasing.

19. DINING ROOM
HAMMOND-HARWOOD HOUSE, ANNAPOLIS, MARYLAND
1770-1774

IN ANNAPOLIS, the capital of Maryland and the first important cultural center south of Philadelphia during Colonial times, domestic architecture shows an even stronger trend to a direct importation of English ideas and the manorial scale of living. Its wealth came chiefly from the tobacco trade which kept it in close touch with England whence a great part of its luxuries were naturally imported, as shown by ancient inventories and advertisements.

An excellent example of the Maryland type is the Hammond-Harwood house built for Matthias Hammond, a lawyer and planter, by William Buckland just prior to the Revolution. Its architecture shows Buckland's mature ability as a designer. This interior, while undoubtedly influenced by the rococo modifications widely publicized in Abraham Swan's "British Architect" of 1745, shows more of that Palladian spaciousness which characterizes the best Georgian building.

In this miniature reproduction the design of the chimney breast, the elaborate headings of the doors and windows, and the coffer paneling of the shutters are indications of the differences between the southern and northern adaptations of Georgian design. While generally less refined in detail, the southern interiors have a more spacious and monumental quality which reflects both the climate and the manner of life.

Since at present the house lacks its original furnishings, reproductions of some of the finest pieces of American furniture in the Sheraton style belonging to eastern museums have been used to recreate the atmosphere of such a home during the last years of the century. A particularly southern adjunct to the sideboard is the mixing table standing between the two doors.

The house has now become the property of the Hammond-Harwood House Association, Inc. whose purpose it is to furnish it suitably and make it available to the general public as a museum. It should be noted that in order to increase the effectiveness of the model the original arrangement of this room has been radically altered.

20. DINING ROOM

GUNSTON HALL, FAIRFAX COUNTY, VIRGINIA

1758

Near the potomac river, a few miles from Mount Vernon, stands Gunston Hall, the home of George Mason, known as the author of the Bill of Rights. It was here that George Mason and Thomas Jefferson are thought to have worked on the first draft of the Declaration of Independence.

The interior architecture of Gunston Hall is notably individual. The designs and their execution are attributed to William Buckland, a talented young English master carpenter and builder, who came to America in 1755 under a contract of indenture to George Mason's brother, Thomson Mason. Gunston Hall was completed in 1758, and its spacious and stately rooms earned such praise for Buckland that he was given many commissions in Annapolis and his future success assured.

The hallway and living rooms of Gunston Hall have the greatest distinction. The room which we have chosen to reproduce in miniature is generally considered one of the most interesting designs in the eighteenth century "Chinese taste" in America. Architecturally this is evident principally in the treatment of the cornices or headings of the overmantel and of the doors and windows where brackets are introduced to carry Chinese figurines or porcelains. In actuality today, the walls are plain, but when the house was built wallpaper was much in vogue, and it is likely that the use of Chinese wallpaper such as is here reproduced was intended.

Unfortunately there is no record of its original furnishings but the Chinese taste was doubtless represented in its Chippendale version as it is in these miniature replicas. The center table is of a later type introduced at the end of the century. In "Chinese" Chippendale the earlier cabriole leg is replaced by a straight leg of rectangular or clustered section. It is possible that the original furnishings were those of a bedroom instead of a dining room. The sideboard shown is a modern version of Chinese Chippendale.

21. THE WEST PARLOR
MOUNT VERNON, FAIRFAX COUNTY, VIRGINIA
1743-1799

THE HOME OF George Washington, probably the most famous Colonial house in America, is by no means architecturally the finest. It has, however, in addition to its unique historic significance the virtue of being a typical example of the average larger Virginia manor. Washington, like his fellow gentlemen planters, considered it proper to take more than a passive interest in architecture and the planning of his own house. Like other distinguished Americans of his day, it is probable that to all intents and purposes he was his own architect.

The property had been in the hands of the Washington family for eighty-three years before it was inherited by the First President. He began to enlarge and improve the original house shortly before his marriage to Martha Custis, the work continuing sporadically until his death.

The changes made by Washington indicate that his tastes lay toward the somewhat heavy Palladian classic forms favored by most of his contemporaries. The doorway shown in this model of the West Parlor is an instance. Otherwise the room with its raised paneling is part of the older home. The corner fireplace has a mantel and overmantel of mid-eighteenth century type, the arms introduced between the scrolls of the pediment being those of the Washington family.

The model is furnished to suggest the appointments of the room during the later years of Washington's occupancy. The pieces are mostly reproductions of fine Sheraton examples. A so-called Martha Washington high back, upholstered chair stands beside the mantel. The silver tray holding the Lowestoft tea set is a replica of one of Madam Washington's prized possessions. The rug reproduces one of the French Aubusson carpets which were presented to George Washington.

The portrait seen through the door is a reproduction of a famous work by Gilbert Stuart, Washington at Dorchester Heights.

Through the windows may be seen the lawn leading to the Potomac and also a glimpse of the colonnade connecting the mansion with the offices.

While Washington lived in Mount Vernon hardly a day passed without the presence of guests. On mild days much entertaining took place on the broad veranda looking across the lawn to the river and the green slopes beyond.

22. DINING ROOM
KENMORE, FREDERICKSBURG, VIRGINIA
1750-1758

In 1752 when George Washington's sister Betty married Colonel Fielding Lewis, they went to Fredericksburg, Virginia, to live in their stately home, Kenmore, which had just been completed. We have no record of the architect of Kenmore so it is probable that Colonel Lewis directed the work with the aid of English books on architecture and the services of a trained master builder.

The exterior of this square Georgian house is of red brick with white trim, but the interior is unlike any of the other houses of the locality. This is due to the extraordinarily rich plasterwork of the ceilings and over-mantels completed later in the century. There are two legends regarding this work. One is that a Frenchman who had been employed in the Palace of Versailles was commissioned to design the ornamental stucco at both Kenmore and Mount Vernon. The other version is that Hessian prisoners, captured at Trenton, New Jersey, were sent by General Washington to his sister's house to complete the stucco relief which he is said to have suggested. Unfortunately for romance both these stories have little foundation in fact.

In order to show these unusual features to the best advantage in the model, the dining room ceiling has been copied with the overmantel of the smaller of the drawing rooms. The architectural adornment of the room is concentrated in this plasterwork which renders it all the more effective. The style of the plasterwork suggests a date one or two decades later than that of the house itself. It shows the influence of the early work of the brothers Adam and an acquaintance with Batty Langley's "Builder's Treasury" of 1750.

The great elegance of these rooms of Kenmore calls for the finest examples of American furniture. For this dining room copies of distinguished pieces from museums and private collections have been made. They are mostly in the Hepplewhite-Sheraton style which was introduced into this country after the Revolution and therefore do not represent the original furnishings which must have followed earlier Georgian forms.

The windows open on a broad portico with white columns. Across a garden is a glimpse of the exterior of Kenmore so that the visitor may visualize this charming mansion over which Betty Washington Lewis presided.

The Kenmore Association has been formed to protect this historic home and to preserve it for future generations.

23. DRAWING-ROOM
WILTON, HENRICO COUNTY, VIRGINIA
1754

THE ESTATES on the south River Road out of Richmond are rich in history, tradition and romance. One of the nearest to Richmond was Wilton, built in the mid-eighteenth century for William Randolph III.

Some acquaintance with the principles of architecture was considered a necessary part of the equipment of a cultured gentleman of the eighteenth century. Though possibly accompanied by some knowledge of building, the services of a trained craftsman, usually a master mason, were necessary to turn it to practical account. In fact, it is to these master craftsmen, filling the modern functions of architect and contractor, that most of the credit for the enduring qualities of eighteenth century architecture in America must be given. As in most cases, the real author of Wilton remains anonymous, yet the fine proportions of the exterior and the elegance of the interior prove his talents to have been of a high order.

The drawing-room reproduced here is a fine example of the completely paneled room. The fireplace end is dignified by the introduction of fluted pilasters and flanking arches which in the original partly mask windows which were set inconveniently close to the chimney. The marble mantel is of a type introduced into England from the Continent and adopted occasionally in the South. The rather elaborate plasterwork of the ceiling is unusual and is probably a somewhat later addition. The model shows some minor deviations from the original in detail and disposition.

The furniture consists principally of reproductions of pieces in the Queen Anne style which retained its popularity in this country until after the middle of the century. The "Japanned" highboy shows the result of the "Chinese taste" which had an extensive vogue in this country following its popularity throughout Europe.

Wilton, like other southern rooms in this series, points to the luxury and comfort enjoyed by the rich planters long before the Revolution. Ships brought the latest fashions of Europe to their river landings. The difficulties of land travel were relieved by water transportation and contact with their neighbors for "routs" and the hunt was relatively easy. With numerous servants, white as well as negro, at their call, the landed gentry of Virginia lived on a scale rivaling, if not surpassing, that of their equals in England.

In 1935 Wilton was moved to West Hampton just outside Richmond. It is now the property of The Society of Colonial Dames of America. It has been restored and furnished and is open to the public during certain hours.

24. ENTRANCE HALL
CARTER'S GROVE, JAMES CITY COUNTY, VIRGINIA
1751

THE NAME TIDEWATER has become almost synonymous with eastern Virginia. In early Colonial days the great plantations were developed along the lower reaches of the rivers where the tides permitted shipments of cotton, rice, and tobacco to be floated down to the ports along the coast and transshipped to Europe. Most of the planters' mansions on the Tidewater were Georgian in character and we find the majority of the finest examples on the James River and around Williamsburg.

It is said that the outstanding qualities of a Georgian home are spaciousness, balanced scale, and gracious dignity. Carter's Grove possesses all of these. Crowning a bluff eighty feet above the James River, surrounded by a sweep of thickly turfed lawn and fine old trees, this handsome brick home stands today as a symbol of the security and comfort which attended life on the great southern estates up to the Civil War.

Carter Burwell, a descendant of the famous "King" Carter, commissioned the English builder, David Minitree, to build Carter's Grove in 1751. The house was completed within the year and it became a center of social activity in that romantic period of stagecoaches, cavaliers and lovely ladies bedecked in frills of lace and rich damasks.

On opening the front door one enters a hall with superb paneling of native walnut lately restored from under layers of paint applied by former owners. The stairway, one of the most notable features of the home, is famed in the historical and architectural annals of Virginia.

The furniture used in the model follows designs fashionable in England during the reign of George I and produced by Philadelphia cabinetmakers up to the middle of the century. They mark a transition between the true Queen Anne forms and those sponsored by Thomas Chippendale.

This plantation was ravaged by the British during the Revolution. The greatest scars were made by Tarleton's dragoons who slashed the handrail with their sabers while riding their horses up the grand staircase for diversion. The marks are visible today. The house at that time is thought to have been headquarters for the English.

25. DRAWING-ROOM
CARTER'S GROVE, JAMES CITY COUNTY, VIRGINIA
1751

THE MANY COUNTRIES of Europe have distinctively national types of domestic architecture, while we have no unified, coordinated American pattern. Our different states were established by different kinds of people who thought differently and lived differently. Some were wealthy landowners, others merchants and shippers, and they came to America from foreign lands. These conditions were naturally reflected in the designs of their houses, for the tendency to translate what Europe sent us runs continuously through our handicrafts and our architecture.

In the South, particularly in Virginia, where wealth and culture were combined with a strong English manorial tradition, the Colonial Georgian house reached its greatest elegance. Carter's Grove may well be taken as the archetype of the eighteenth century Virginia mansion.

This southeast drawing-room is completely paneled in walnut which, through the action of time, has attained a wonderfully soft tone of red-brown. The paneling follows the usual "raised" form with a boldly beveled edge. It is simple and well proportioned. The effectiveness of the design lies in the mantel treatment, plain panels above a facing of Siena marble surrounded by a full Tuscan Doric order beautifully carved and proportioned.

Through the door into the hall the woodwork and dado are seen to be painted a rich green, a shade much used in this part of the country.

The furniture in the model reproduces fine Chippendale types of mixed English and American design such as might well have found a place in the room prior to the Revolution. The center chandelier is copied from one owned by the Metropolitan Museum. The "bull's-eye" mirror over the fireplace is of a definitely later type.

26. DINING ROOM
A "JEFFERSONIAN" HOUSE, VIRGINIA (T)
ABOUT 1800

THOMAS JEFFERSON, statesman and political philosopher, the author of the Declaration of Independence and third president of the United States, was also an architect by avocation and inclination.

Architecture and its problems were among his chief interests throughout his life. The influence of this interest was felt far beyond Virginia and the charming buildings of the University of Virginia at Charlottesville are today a monument to his talents as a designer.

A smaller but no less distinguished monument is Jefferson's own home, Monticello, a red brick structure with colonnaded porticoes, white balustrades and trim, standing on the summit of a spur of the Blue Ridge Mountains overlooking the Rivanna River. His devotion to the place is expressed in his own words, "All my wishes end where I hope my days will end, at Monticello." Begun in 1772, Monticello was not completed until 1808.

In addition to his intense interest in architecture as such, Jefferson had a passion for ingenious gadgets, a taste by no means unique even in his time, and indulged this freely in the design of his own house.

The main purpose in this model is to show this very human side of the great man through the devices installed in his dining room at Monticello. The room is by no means a reproduction of that in Monticello as, outside of these devices, it is extremely simplified and definitely rearranged.

The mantel is a replica of the original which is equipped with doors in the side communicating directly with the wine cellar below. The window on the left is hung in three sections or sashes, a most flexible arrangement for control of ventilation. The folding doors in the rear leading to a replica of the "tea room" of Monticello are also said to be one of Jefferson's own contrivances.

Though the original furnishings of Monticello are now mostly dispersed, the model has been equipped in accordance with what Jefferson might have used. The banquet table in the center is, in fact, a reproduction of one designed and owned by Jefferson. Its style naturally leads to the Sheraton-Empire types of the Duncan Phyfe chairs and consoles which accompany it.

The crystal chandelier and brackets are copies of examples in the Metropolitan Museum, New York City, and the crystal table ornaments are replicas of a notable English set.

The needlepoint rug is of a simple Empire pattern of French make of a type much used in the South.

27. KITCHEN

GOVERNOR'S PALACE, WILLIAMSBURG, VIRGINIA

18TH CENTURY

IN THEIR RESTORATION of the ancient capital of Virginia the architects and their associates have given us as complete a picture of the life of the Colony as tradition checked by exhaustive research can possibly create.

This restoration of the kitchen of the Governor's Palace shows us what this heart of the southern domestic economy looked like in the eighteenth century. Unlike the kitchen or living room of the ancient New England home, the offices or kitchen were placed in a separate wing or pavilion where the colored domestics and their offspring could swarm without disturbing the master's family. With this exception there is little essential difference. The heart of the room is the great open fireplace with its hanging crane and "dutch" oven for baking before an open fire, simple appurtenances for concocting those delicacies for which the southern cooks became famous. Most of the cooking utensils of metal were homemade in the plantation smithy and hence have that handwrought quality which gives them a certain individual charm.

In themselves the furnishings have a nondescript quaintness which came from the use of sturdy survivals of an earlier day together with strictly utilitarian pieces.

The ladder-like stair leads to a storeroom. The servants had their own cabins at a distance from the house.

Through the doorway is a glimpse of an old-fashioned vegetable and herb garden and outside the window is the iron kettle in which soft soap was boiled. At the back of the garden were the smokehouses where the famous Virginia hams and bacon were cured.

28. DRAWING-ROOM
A HOUSE IN CHARLESTON, SOUTH CAROLINA (T)
1775-1800

UP TO THE CIVIL WAR Charleston was the acknowledged center of the social and commercial life of the South Atlantic states. In spite of its commercial interests the tone of the city was largely set by the wealthy planters whose town mansions became the center of social activity. It was on their town houses rather than on those on the plantation that the owners lavished most of their care and taste, so these houses became in fact embodiments of the best architectural and decorative skill of the old South.

Although Charleston was an early settlement, practically nothing has survived previous to 1740 when a great fire demolished most of the town, and subsequent disasters have taken their toll of what was left. The chief periods of prosperity and building preceded and followed the Revolution. The best of the Charleston heritage has survived from these eras, roughly, 1750-1775 and 1800-1830.

This model has been constructed largely on the basis of the detail of the Colonel John Stuart house built in 1772 and altered and enlarged early in the last century. The original woodwork of the second floor drawing-room, from which the doorways and mantel of the model are copied, and that of the dining room are now in the Minneapolis Institute of Arts. The very definite English character of the detail in the modified Palladianism of Abraham Swan's "British Architect" reflects the fact that Charleston's cultural contacts at the time were with the West Indies and England rather than with the other Colonies on the Atlantic seaboard.

In its arrangement the model is a composite of the original drawing-room and a late addition built over the garden and used as a dining room. This accounts for the bay, a Victorian motif, which while dramatically effective and reflecting what actually happened in many older houses, perforce detracts from the "period" purity of the setting.

The room is furnished with replicas of Sheraton and Hepplewhite pieces of both English and American models. Charleston's contacts with the Orient is indicated by the presence of Chinese rugs and a remarkable replica of a lacquer screen executed by a noted Chinese craftsman.

By and large the model represents the spirit of the first of the two Charleston periods mentioned above.

29. BALLROOM
A HOUSE IN CHARLESTON, SOUTH CAROLINA (T)
1775-1835

CHARLESTON HOUSES were designed with many storied galleries running across the side facing the prevailing breeze, frequently at right angles to the street. Numerous French doors opened out on these galleries to take advantage of every movement in the air. Also, for the sake of coolness, the rooms were made as large as possible with high ceilings and many openings to encourage circulation. The main room, a large drawing-room or ballroom, was usually found on the second floor for the same reason. The main entrance was generally at the street end of the first floor gallery. This arrangement is peculiar to Charleston where the galleries or piazzas were used as rooms and privacy was highly valued. Through the windows of this model can be seen the white trimmed front door and the outside galleries of the neighboring house across the garden with its palm trees and azaleas.

This model is composed of motifs taken from the Gibbes-Sloan house (1775) and the Radcliffe-King house (1806) in order to show the great elegance of the large Charleston homes of the early nineteenth century.

The "Palladian" window from the King house is a favorite Charleston motif but is usually a feature of a central hall rather than a room. The columns are based on those in the stair hall of the Gibbes house. The entire treatment reflects the popularity of the Adam style in post-Revolutionary Charleston.

Of the material prosperity and hospitality of the people of the city, Josiah Quincy of Massachusetts wrote in his diary as early as 1773: "This town makes a beautiful appearance as you come up to it, and in many respects, a magnificent one. I can only say that in grandeur, splendor of buildings, decoration and equipages, it far surpasses all I can ever expect to see in America."

Indicating both their popularity in the South and their appropriateness to a room of this character, the furnishings used are mainly in the so-called American Empire or Regency style which was in vogue chiefly between 1810 and 1840. The black lacquer or dark mahogany ground of these pieces is effectively relieved by the gilded ornament in which the lion and the eagle each plays a prominent part. The work of Duncan Phyfe of New York exemplifies the style at its best.

30. DOUBLE PARLOR
HOUSE OF A GEORGIA PLANTER (T)
ABOUT 1850

THE GREAT PROSPERITY of the Deep South came approximately at the time of the western expansion when the Greek Revival was at its height. The Greek portico and temple façade were in fact rather more suited to the climate and spaciousness of southern life than to conditions in the northern and middle western states.

Behind the planter's mansion with its columned facade were other buildings often connected with the "Big House" by open arcades. In these quarters the colored servants cooked and attended to other household activities. Great plantations were of necessity self-sustaining and among the many slaves were artisans of all types. There were blacksmiths, tinners, carpenters, all trained to their trades. The common labor was furnished by the "hands" brought in from the fields between seasons.

In these houses economy of space was of little consideration. Protection from the summer heat was the main object. High ceilings and free circulation of air were called for and to this end the majority of plantation houses were built around a large central hall running from front to back and containing the main staircase. On one side were the front and back parlors connected through wide openings with double doors.

These plantations were often far apart. Roads were bad and travel tedious. A generous hospitality was almost obligatory and when guests came they usually spent a few days, often many weeks. There were "visitors' quarters," sometimes as many as fifty rooms arranged for friends and relatives, and one can imagine what activities weddings and balls would bring to the usually self-contained life of these abundant households.

This model is intended to give a composite picture of an interior in a typical southern late Greek Revival house of the era preceding the Civil War. The mantel, the ponderous carved gold mirrors, elaborately draped curtains and the ornate decorations show the style of the period. The Wilton carpet, often covering the entire floor, could never be too gay in design, nor could the furniture have sufficient clusters of fruit and flowers. It was an effulgent era, an era of wealth, sparkle and generous hospitality not unaptly expressed in the rather ill-organized yet warm-hearted elaborations of the Victorian taste.

In this reproduction the object in view was to select the best of the epoch, not to caricature it, for there is a fine, solid dignity in the southern adaptation of a style which Queen Victoria made the fashion on both sides of the Atlantic.

31. ENTRANCE HALL
THE HERMITAGE, NEAR NASHVILLE, TENNESSEE
1835-1845

THOUGH, in the eyes of the plutocracy of the Atlantic Coast, General Andrew Jackson, seventh president of the United States, became almost a symbol of the unruly democracy of the West, he was in fact one of the aristocracy of the South, a planter and landed proprietor with a passionate interest in the breeding of fine horses. He was a firm believer in the elegance of life proper to his station and in 1835 engaged two journeymen builders, Joseph Rieff and William C. Hume, to rebuild The Hermitage along the lines of the old house destroyed by fire.

This is the house that stands today substantially as it did in the days of Old Hickory. Though acquired by Tennessee from Jackson's impoverished heirs not long after his death as a memorial to her most eminent son, it gradually fell into decay until comparatively recently when it was reconditioned. Fortunately much of its original furnishings, long dispersed through the neighborhood, were collected and reinstalled.

The house, consisting of a central porticoed pavilion with flanking wings, is typical of Greek Revival design. The interior is not elaborate as this simple hall shows. The spiral staircase, apparently self-supporting in its graceful flying curve, is, however, very representative of the style.

The walls of the hall are covered with a scenic wallpaper similar to the one used in the model which is copied from a contemporary set in the collections of The Art Institute of Chicago. The furniture is reproduced from pieces used by the Jackson family.

Through a door to the left a corner of General Jackson's study may be glimpsed, his portrait hanging above his own desk and chairs in replica. The unusual lustered hanging lamp in the hall is worthy of notice.

It is recorded that General Jackson was greatly attached to this house where he spent the happiest days of his life. He and his wife, Rachel, are buried beneath a temple-like monument in its gardens.

32. BEDROOM
A HOUSE IN NEW ORLEANS, LOUISIANA (T)
1800-1850

NEW ORLEANS is more or less of a "sport" among American cities. Founded among the swamps of the Mississippi delta, it commands one of the greatest inland waterways of the world and was the key to an inland empire contested by the Spaniards, the French and the infant United States during one of the most romantic epochs in history. The rendezvous of adventurers of every race and the silent partner of pirates, it early acquired an aura of picaresque romance which has survived and even been confirmed amid the political vicissitudes of our own day.

In the old city, the Vieux Carré, much of its ancient architecture, the battered remnant of its Franco-Spanish (Creole) culture, has also survived. Even more successfully, the traditions of a world-renowned culinary art persist; for whatever its artistic losses, New Orleans has always kept its food.

In its houses the Vieux Carré has something that recalls those of the French West Indies, and more remotely, those of Mediterranean France, but the builders were probably guided more directly by the handbooks of Asher Benjamin and Minard Lafever. A subtropical climate with high humidity and a water-soaked ground called for shade and ample ventilation. Enclosed courtyards, high ceilings and lacy cast and wrought iron balconies climbing over many stories were the natural outcome of all these factors.

Great prosperity only briefly interrupted by the War of 1812 came to New Orleans after the Louisiana Purchase of 1803. Most of its finest houses date from this period when the Greek Revival mingled with echoes of the French Empire and the late Georgian styles. Enormous quantities of furniture and luxuries from Europe, France, and England undoubtedly found their way to the city during those years when "Cotton was King," only to be dispersed and destroyed during the Civil War and the unhappy years that followed.

This model is designed to give a composite picture of a boudoir and bedroom in a fine New Orleans residence of the second quarter of the last century. The mantel follows one in the Girod house in the old city. The door and window trim is copied from that in the Hurst plantation on the city's outskirts and the delicate cornice is that of the Forsyth house in the Garden District. Through the long French windows of the bay is an indication of the cast-iron railings of a typical balcony. The furniture, somewhat later than the room itself, shows the heavy mahogany of the American Empire style so popular in the South mingling with pieces which reflect the black and gold elegance of the French taste of the time of Louis-Philippe.

33. PARLOR
A HOUSE IN "MIDDLETOWN" (T)
1875-1900

THIS GROUP of parlor, hall and dining room will bring a gleam to the eyes that is not all of amusement, for this is the background against which most of us now admitting middle age passed the memorable days of our childhood. Here and there we still may see these houses, which owned no textbook style but boasted the proudest efforts of the carpenter and his scroll saw on porch and verge board. "Gothic" of pointed window, tortured "Queen Anne" and hints of Oriental dreams mingled in friendly fashion with remnants of classic dignity.

Inside, brown and its parents green and maroon were the prevailing notes. A vaguely awesome hallway wherein that strange tree, the hallrack, blossomed with footgear and apparel according to season, gave into darksome passages above and below filled with unexpected obstacles. On one side opened the everyday parlor or living room as distinct from the sacredly portentous Sunday parlor with its chosen *lares and penates* open only on special occasions. Beyond it opened the dining room where the table was always set with white cloth, colored glass, pickle dishes and the ever present condiment castor. Here at mealtime the "hired girl" brought in steaming dishes and put them in convenient places around the board. The head of the family carved; and it was not a disgrace to ask for a "second helping" for in those days dieting was for invalids and a well upholstered figure was an asset.

As we see it there was not a piece of furniture in the entire place that had good lines. It was the age of knick-knacks with the "whatnot" and the cabinet and every other available space filled with family souvenirs and the trophies of the Centennial Exposition. The Rogers Group, the crayon enlargement and perhaps a hand-painted oil were art and quantity was king. It was a chattery conglomeration yet friendly and cheerful in spite of the drab plaids that bore up under hard family use. The patent rocker and its simple cousin swayed in varying and soothing rhythm on porch and in parlor as the seasons turned and the stove was set up and dismantled before the befrilled coal grate. The photograph appears in album and on the wall. Here to the left of the fireplace hangs one of Abraham Lincoln and his son, Tad, a rare treasure-trove from some admirer's locket. Note the paper rack on the opposite side.

In such rooms, in spite of machine carving and horrors in cast metal, reigned the spirit of home that plastics and chromium find hard to entice. Here behind portiere and Gothic window was the refuge of leisure caught for a while by knob and tassel before being blown away by the winds of speed and their servants, the automobile and telephone.

34. DINING ROOM
A HOUSE IN NEW MEXICO (T)
CONTEMPORARY

DURING THE SIXTEENTH CENTURY Spanish adventurers led expeditions into the New World, establishing themselves in Mexico where they acquired vast fortunes. In 1540 Coronado at the head of a large force penetrated the unknown desert lands of what is now Santa Fe. Though these early conquerors built nothing which remained for future generations, their successors left a tradition and a way of life that has largely endured to our time.

Even more tangible reminders of the Spanish occupation have been left in and around the ancient city of San Antonio. The old missions tell us of the intrepid padres who were the pioneers of western civilization, and other ancient buildings remind us of those adventurous dons whose colorful lives threw a halo of romance over a large part of the Southwest when it was still part of the empire of old Spain.

The structure of this model New Mexican dining room follows closely that of the hallway in the ancient palace of the Spanish governors in San Antonio. In feeling it shows itself essentially Spanish, yet expressed with materials and methods native to the Pueblo Indians. The walls, three feet thick, are made of adobe bricks of sun-dried clay. These are laid in mud mortar and are mud-plastered inside and out. Whitewash is then applied, sometimes in pinkish or cream tones. The roofs are of heavy projecting beams. Earth is tamped down upon a wooden ceiling made of small saplings laid "herring-bone" fashion upon larger beams. The floors are of tile or earth, stained with ox blood or paint and polished. Corner fireplaces are very characteristic and inside these the piñon wood is stacked in Indian fashion. Through the window is shown a cactus garden and beyond an Indian pueblo, so familiar in the deserts of New Mexico where these great hive-like dwellings house many Indian families.

The furniture in this room is copied from pieces used in modern New Mexican houses. It is both Spanish and Mexican in character. The tin shrine and candle sconces are Mexican designs. The old silver, pottery and rugs were found in the City of Mexico.

35. LIVING ROOM
GEORGE WASHINGTON SMITH HOUSE, SANTA BARBARA, CALIFORNIA
CONTEMPORARY

BOTH HERITAGE and climate form a basis for the continuation of the Spanish Colonial tradition in the southern portion of California. The mission style was evolved to meet the needs and limitations of the first white settlers just as the wooden architecture of early New England was the result of the adaptation of English traditions to the requirements and materials of the new land.

In Santa Barbara, dominated by its famous Franciscan Mission built in 1820, and unrestricted by the pressure of modern industrialism, the Spanish tradition is a particularly logical source of inspiration. Its subtropical climate both permits and calls for the open patio, the heavy walls and the colorful materials which stem more or less directly from the mingling of Moorish and Latin elements in old Spain.

This room is a reproduction in miniature of the living room of the home of George Washington Smith, an architect who was eminently successful in the adaptation of the Spanish Colonial style to contemporary use. Its design suggests rather than copies the traditional forms, though the ceiling follows closely the timber work of the Hispano-Moresque builders. The furniture reproduces types characteristic of Spain from the fifteenth to the eighteenth centuries.

The success of the architect lay in his ability to infuse his designs with the romantic quality of the style without sacrificing the comfort and convenience demanded today. The Smith home is widely conceded to be one of the most representative of its type.

36. LIVING ROOM
SOBERANES HOUSE, MONTEREY, CALIFORNIA
1850-1875

DURING the decade of 1830-1840 an era of prosperity began for the Golden State. To Monterey, the capital and a fine seaport, came adventurous New Englanders in their clipper ships, bringing their wives and families on the dangerous journey around the Horn to settle in the new land.

In the houses of early Monterey we find in consequence an interesting mingling of New England tradition with what may be called native Spanish elements. Sundried adobe brick was used for walls three feet thick, an excellent insulation; and Victorian furniture brought in the holds of the clippers to soften the homesickness of the Yankee settlers was mixed with pieces of Spanish flavor.

The usual plan of these houses was well adapted to the simple and hospitable life which existed in California a century ago. On the ground floor were a living room, a dining room and a kitchen and storeroom. All the bedrooms were on the second floor and were reached by an outside stairway to an upper balcony which ran across the side of the house.

Such a Spanish balcony may be seen through the door of this model on the house beyond the adobe garden wall. Wanting less romantic atmosphere and more comfort, the Yankees had their stairs built inside like those in their old homes.

Tiles were often used on the floors of the earliest houses but with the arrival of the new settlers came round-dancing and a more suitable wooden floor was built into many homes. The "sala" or ballroom then became popular.

To give an accurate example of the old Monterey type of house this model follows the living room of the Soberanes house. Here the smooth plaster walls are white. The inside shutters, sill and trim are painted light yellow ochre. The wide boards of the pine floor are stained dark brown. The wooden mantel, reminiscent of New England in its split spindle and turned ornament, is painted black and set on a raised hearth.

37. HALLWAY
A PENTHOUSE APARTMENT, SAN FRANCISCO, CALIFORNIA (T)
CONTEMPORARY

THIS MODEL follows no actual example and is not intended to offer any suggestions as to a proper approach to modern design. Its purpose is merely to indicate the general character of a modern room designed as an appropriate background for contemporary works of art and to point out what may well be called the international quality of design today.

The walls are painted a neutral tone to show off to best advantage the remarkable miniature originals painted by well-known contemporary artists and representing such modern pictures as may well be acquired by a collector in such a cosmopolitan center as San Francisco.

On the wall to the left is a tiny painting in gouache by Jean Victor Hugo, Au bord de la mer. Hugo, born in 1894, is a grandson of the famous poet and represents the modern "primitivist" school. Beyond the door to the terrace is a crayon drawing by Marie Laurencin, Promenade dans la forêt, formerly in the collection of Paul Guillaume. Two bronze groups by John Storrs, the contemporary American sculptor born in 1885, stand in curtained window recesses on either side of the fireplace. On the chimney breast a miniature masterpiece by Amédée Ozenfant represents the work of one of the leaders of the post-cubist movement. In the recess in the right wall hangs a typical work by the famous Fernand Léger, born in 1881, and on the walls to the right and left of this are groups of tiny originals by Léopold Survage, one of the leaders of the contemporary abstractionist movement, born in 1879.

The above works by Léger, Ozenfant, and Survage were made specially for use in this room.

The furniture is of the simplest variety, showing the use of a modern glasslike plastic in the chairs and the decorative function of veneers in the low table fronting the couch. The rug was specially woven by the V'Soske Shops.

Through the French doors is a view of the city including part of "Treasure Island" and a glimpse of the new bridge as seen with its sparkling lights at night.